KEY WEST AND THE SPANISH-AMERICAN WAR

WRIGHT LANGLEY
JOAN LANGLEY

LANGLEY PRESS, INC.
Key West, Florida

Copyright © 1998 by Wright & Joan Langley

Library of Congress Catalog Card Number: 97-92760

ISBN 0-911607-11-0

All rights reserved. No portion of this book may be reproduced in any manner without written permission except for brief quotes for review purposes. For information, please contact the publisher.

First Edition, 1998

Book Design: Joan Langley
Cover Production: Solares Hill Design Group
Graphics Mentor: J.T. Thompson

ILLUSTRATION CREDITS:

Photographs and sketches used in this book are from the collection of Wright Langley or are from the following sources as listed: Marlene Carbonell, page 50, top; Bob Cerkleski, pages 42 top, 66; Frederic Remington Art Museum, page 10; Florida Historical Society, page 41; *Harper's Weekly*, pages 12, 13, 27, 42, 45, 46 top, 48 all, 51; Janet Hayes, page 19; Jewish Historical Society of South Florida, page 18; Key West Art and Historical Society, pages 25 top, 37; *Leslie's Weekly*, pages 8, 47 bottom; Library of Congress, page 22 top, 26, 40, 56; Monroe County Public Library, pages 3, 4, 6, 30, 39, 62 bottom; Naval Historical Foundation, page 36; Connie Phillips, page 30 bottom.; Robert L. White, page 50 bottom.

COVER:

Both covers utilize designs from sheet music published at the time of the Spanish-American War and are from the Joseph Albertson Collection of Spanish-American War Sheet Music at Monroe County Public Library.

LANGLEY PRESS, INC.
821 Georgia Street
Key West, FL 33040
305-294-3156

For our son and daughter,

MARK & LISA LANGLEY

—this one's for you!

Foreword

Many fine books have been published on the Spanish-American War, most of which cover both the Atlantic and the Pacific theaters of the War. This book has a much narrower focus, that of Key West—a small town caught up in a world-altering event.

It is a book that has been years in the making, for it started at Boston University in 1960. While studying for his master's degree in journalism, Wright did a report, "The Pulitzer-Hearst War and the Spanish-American War—A Study of Yellow Journalism from 1896-1900." Both of us became fascinated with the research because, there in the Boston Public Library, in musty old copies of the *New York World* and *New York Herald*, were illustrated articles datelined Key West—Joan's hometown.

Over the years, we collected books, images, and articles on Key West. Many had to do with the Spanish-American War. In 1995, with the 100th anniversary of the war coming up, we looked over our collection and began to plan this book.

We have had much help with our research. We would especially like to thank authors G. J. A. O'Toole, John Edwards Weems, and Michael Blow for their books—and their answers to specific questions—which provided such comprehensive insight into the events of the war and the era. Special thanks also go to Sister Dolores Wehle, Sisters of the Holy Names of Jesus and Mary, who brought us copies of the Convent Hospital records, letters, and photographs from Albany, New York.

Many others deserve our thanks: Laura Branstetter, Marlene Carbonell, Bob Cerkleski, Bill Edwards, Art Espinola, Winifred Fryzel, Adolph Gucinski, Mike Hager, Janet Hayes, Tom Knowles, Rufus Langley, Ed Little, Connie Phillips, Gerald E. Poyo, Bill Reilly, Stephan Vaeth, Glenn Westfall, and Robert L. White.

Because copies of Key West newspapers published during the

Spanish-American War were not available, we relied heavily on the *Florida Times-Union* and its reports filed from Key West. This part of our research was made much easier by the efforts of Tom and Lynda Hambright of the Local and State History Department of the Monroe County Public Library in Key West. The Hambrights have spent hundreds of tedious hours going through microfilm rolls of the Jacksonville newspaper, making and organizing copies of all articles relating to Key West to provide a record of Key West history that has long been missing. They are due special thanks for that and for sharing their knowledge of the period with us.

We have entered the digital age with this book, for it has been produced on computer, in-house, and sent to the printer on disk. Working with the images has been a challenge, for most are 100 years old. Some are screened images taken from newspapers, others are photographs that have faded and spotted with age. A few of the images are of very poor quality, but they have been included because of their historical significance.

We hope you enjoy our effort.

WRIGHT & JOAN LANGLEY
December 1, 1997

Contents

Foreword 5

   I. Key West, April 1898 9

  II. Cuba's Struggle for Independence 12

 III. The Battleship 23

 IV. An Explosion in Havana Harbor 29

   V. Waiting for War 37

 VI. The First Shot 44

VII. Wartime Key West 49

VIII. End of the War 57

 IX. Monuments & Memories 63

Bibliography 70

Key West had the highest population in Florida—18,080 to Jacksonville's 17,201 and Tampa's 5,582—going into the 1890s. This map, published in Leslie's Weekly, *shows the strategic location of Key West as a U.S. naval station and coaling depot.*

I

KEY WEST, APRIL 1898

Early in 1898, Key West became the focus of a world waiting for a war to happen. Because of its proximity to Cuba, scores of writers, photographers, and artists came to the southernmost point in the United States. They came to cover the inevitable—war with Spain.

When the battleship *Maine* blew up in Havana harbor February 15th, war became just a matter of time—time that passed slowly for the waiting journalists.

Richard Harding Davis, distinguished reporter for the *New York Journal*, was among them. With an eye for graphic detail, he captured the flavor of the times and the town in the opening chapter of his book, *The Cuban and Porto Rican Campaigns*:

> It was half-past four on the afternoon of April [21st], and that peace which only exists when the sun is at 103 [degrees overhead] brooded over the coral islands of Key West and over the warships of the North Atlantic Squadron in her bay. The flags at the mast-heads moved irritably in the hot air, the palms at the Custom-house moved not at all, but were cut against the glaring blue sky like giant petals of tin; in the streets the colored drivers slept in their open hacks, and on the porch of the hotel a row of officers in white duck and of correspondents in yachting-caps sat with tilted chairs and with their feet on the railings before them, in a state of depressed and sweltering silence.
>
> For two months they had been waiting at Key West. They had waited while the President's message had be postponed once and three times while Representatives and Senators moved and amended and referred, while foreign powers had offered services more or less friendly, and while all the machinery of diplomacy had been put in motion to avert or

Smartly dressed artists and journalists from throughout the world gathered in Key West to cover the Spanish-American War. Artist Frederic Remington, the man in the white suit and cap on the far right, poses with fellow colleagues beside the Naval Depot building—today's Clinton Market.

to delay the inevitable end. And they had lost hope and interest. For three weeks the White Squadron had been disguised in a warpaint of lead. The decks of the warships had been cleared for action, and the great battleships that were to lead the way, and which stood seven miles nearer to the goal than the others, for three weeks had strained at their anchorage, like dogs struggling in their chains.

Ever since February the 15th, when the *Maine* settled into the mud of Havana Harbor, these men at Key West had held but one desire and one hope, and at half-past four of that hot and peaceful afternoon their reward came.

It wore, when it came, the obvious and commonplace garb of every day. A small boy fell off his bicycle in front of the hotel and ran his eyes along the porch until they rested on a correspondent of the *New York Herald*. To him he handed a telegram, and, mounting his wheel again, rode away up the hot and dusty street. The correspondent opened the envelope with his thumb, and read: "Rain and hail," and started; and then, seeing that the watchful eyes of half the row were upon him, turned his back and took a narrow code-book from his pocket, and ran his finger down its page. He held it toward me, as I stood looking over his shoulder, and I read: "Rain and hail"—"War is declared, fleet ordered to sea."

A few moments later the porch was empty, the hall of the hotel was piled high with hand-bags and sailors' kits, and hack men were lashing their horses down the dusty street; and at water's edge one could see launches, gigs, and cutters streaking the blue surface of the bay with flashes of white and brass; signal flags of brilliant reds and yellows were spreading and fluttering at the signal halyards; wig-waggers beat the air from the bridges, and cross the water, from the decks of the monitors, came the voices of the men answering the roll: "One, two, three, FOUR! One, two, three, FOUR!

Hotel Key West, the large three-story building on the left, was headquarters for the journalists, artists, and photographers who waited for the Spanish-American War to begin. Located on Duval Street beside the First National Bank (today's First Union Bank), it was later known as the Jefferson Hotel.

II

Cuba's Struggle for Independence

The war had been years in the making. Ever since 1823 when an insurrection by the Cuban secret association *Soles de Bolivar* was quelled, Cubans had been actively seeking freedom from an oppressive Spanish government. Insurrections broke out—and were put down—on an almost regular schedule. Instigators and supporters who did not flee the country were either punished or imprisoned.

Many of those who left Cuba settled in Key West, Tampa, Jacksonville, and New York City. Key West, 90 miles from Havana, was the favored location. It had a climate and occupations similar to those the exiles left behind. Here they could make a living in familiar ways and remain in close contact with their fellow compatriots.

When Cuban patriots declared Cuba's independence from Spain with the proclamation *Grito de Yara* in 1868, ten years of bitter fighting began. During the Ten Years War, immigration to Key West increased dramatically and so did the refugees' financial support of revolutions in their homeland. With money earned cigar making, sponging, and fishing, Key West Cubans gave religiously to the cause of freedom. Their American dollars bought guns, ammunition, supplies—and hired boats and crews to take them to Cuba.

Called "filibusters," these expeditions had been going on since the 1840s, and with increasing financial support they became larger and better organized. One filibustering ship typically carried the men and

Shallow-draft boats from the fishing and sponging fleets were used to ferry men and supplies to filibuster vessels anchored off the Florida Keys.

The Jacksonville-based **Dauntless** *served as a filibuster for many years during Cuba's fight for independence from Spain. Known as the "fastest tug in the South," the* **Dauntless** *would often have to outrun U.S. naval vessels patrolling the Florida Keys. When war was declared, the* **Dauntless** *was chartered by the Associated Press "as a dispatch boat to work in connection with the fleet at Key West."*

another, the arms. To avoid violating U.S. neutrality laws, the men and arms were brought together in international waters. Key West and the sparsely inhabited Florida Keys became staging points for expeditions to Cuba.

In 1873 one filibuster's expedition nearly brought the United States into war with Spain. According to naval historian J.R. Mickler:

> The *Virginius*, which by common knowledge was a filibustering ship, was captured by the Spanish on the high seas and taken into Santiago. Although later investigation disclosed that the *Virginius* was fraudulently registered as an American vessel, her captain was an American citizen and there were Americans among the crew and passengers. Indignation at home reached fever pitch when the Santiago authorities court martialled and shot 53 persons from the *Virginius* as pirates, including the captain and other Americans.
>
> The Navy Department rushed every available warship to Key West to prepare for hostilities. These were averted when Spain paid $80,000 in indemnities to the families of the men executed. But national ill-feeling was not assuaged.
>
> In succeeding years, as public sentiment crystallized, the Navy kept one or more warships continually at Key West, partly as a precautionary measure, partly as a token of the

Administration's desire to interrupt filibustering to Cuba in the interests of neutrality.

It was definitely a token measure, for filibustering continued and tensions between Spain and the Cubans intensified. In Key West the mounting tension literally reached a flash point on March 30, 1886 when a suspicious fire started at San Carlos Institute. The Institute was founded in 1871 and was the beloved "Casa Cuba" of those who migrated to Key West. Located at 516 Duval Street in the heart of the city, San Carlos stood not only as a cultural center but as a symbol for the Cuban revolutionary movement.

Pushed by a breeze, the fire soon engulfed the San Carlos and raced out of control. It did not stop until it reached the waterfront. The *Tobacco Leaf*, an industry newspaper published in New York City, reported in the edition of April 3, 1886:

> Key West, Fla.. March 30—This has been a sad day for Key West, the most exclusive cigar city in the country. Today it has a half dozen less large cigar factories than it had yesterday, besides numerous other structures, both business and private. The story is thus told:
>
> A fire started in the San Carlos Theater at 10 o'clock this

Fire raced from San Carlos five blocks away down Duval Street to the water. This bleak scene looking northeast from Front Street toward Duval Street shows the path of the fire. The large building on the far right is still standing at Duval and Greene Streets where Kennedy Studios is located today.

morning [March 30] and soon got beyond the control of the firemen, owing to a fresh wind which was blowing from the south. The Episcopal and Baptist Churches were among the first buildings destroyed. E. H. Gato's residence, which stands just back of the theater, was soon licked by the flames; as were also fifty other buildings including the cigar factories of Seidenberg & Co., Cayetano Soria, E. Canals, Julius Ellinger & Co., H. K. Kelly & Co., J. H. Gregory, J. R. Angulo, Navarro & Co., and Alfonso & Co. The bonded warehouse containing a quarter of a million dollars' worth of Havana tobacco and Wolf's cigar-box factory were also consumed. After burning the first block the fire took a northwesterly course to Elizabeth Street, sweeping everything before it down to the wharves. The heat was so intense that both firemen and sailors were driven back by it. The fire subsided at 3 o'clock, but not until after the principal part of the town had been burned. Six wharves and five brick warehouses were among the structures destroyed. The loss can not be less than $1,500,000, with little insurance, probably not $100,000. About fifteen persons were injured, of whom six were taken to the Marine Hospital and others on board the men-of-war. No lives were lost. Everything in town is in such a state of confusion.

Just over a month later the *Tobacco Leaf*, May 1, 1886, followed up the story with the report:

The several rumors that have been floating around here pointing to the incendiary origin of the late fire are obtaining more foundation day by day, and the truth of them may be proven ere long. Attention is called to the fact that three days before the fire there was a general report in Havana that Key West was burning. This may have been a coincidence, and if it was, it was certainly remarkable. But many people do not believe that it was, and look upon the whole affair with suspicion.

Whether or not the fire had been set at San Carlos to discourage Cubans from supporting the revolution, the fire crippled both the town and the cigar industry. Certainly it cut deeply into contributions from the workers.

Although some families moved away temporarily, Key West bounced back from the fire and began to rebuild. The *Bensel Directory of 1887* reported some 150 cigar factories with a weekly payroll of

Cubans line Government Wharf, preparing to leave Key West after the fire of March 30, 1886. Small boats from a U.S. naval vessel are ferrying them away from the docks at the Naval Depot—today's Clinton Market—in the background. Some Cubans returned to their homeland while others relocated to Tampa until their homes were rebuilt in Key West.

about $50,000 and an annual output of 90 million cigars. The directory also noted that 150 new buildings were being constructed and more were planned. (The red brick U.S. Custom House, Monroe County Courthouse, City Hall on Greene Street, and a new San Carlos Institute were among the buildings constructed in the early 1890s.)

On Christmas Day 1891 the Cuban patriot José Martí arrived from Tampa on the Peninsular and Occidental steamship *Olivette*. "On the pier he was received by an immense multitude of émigrés [with] Cuban and American banners and flags. A musical band accompanied the organization committee in order to receive Martí," one report stated. He had been invited to Key West to help unite the diverse factions of the revolutionary movement.

Martí had joined the Cuban independence movement as a very young man, shortly after the Ten Years War began. He became such a patriot that by the time he was 17, he was arrested and convicted of disloyal activities and sentenced to six years hard labor. He finished his university studies in Spain when he was deported there in 1871 and began a career as a teacher and writer in Mexico, Guatemala, and Venezuela. At the end of the Ten Years War in 1878, he returned to Cuba and was once again deported to Spain because of his fervent revolutionary activity.

In 1881 Martí moved to New York and his reputation as an outspoken and respected orator, writer, and organizer for Cuban independence continued to grow. He became well-known for his opposition to a strictly military revolution that ignored the issues of racial equality and social justice.

Martí was ill on his first trip to Key West, but walked from the pier to the nearby Duval House, located at 119 Duval Street, followed by thousands of his supporters. Forced to rest by a doctor, he had to delay a speech planned for the next day until January 3. On that day San Carlos Institute filled with eager Cubans an hour before his speech and an estimated 5,000 more gathered outside on Duval Street. "His speech was listened to with religious unction, interrupted from time to time with warm applause," a Cuban newspaper reported. During the rest of his stay, he visited and spoke to workers at cigar factories all over town and attended numerous banquets in his honor. At each appearance he exhorted the Cubans to continue to support and fund the movement.

José Martí, the great Cuban leader, called his much loved Key West—"the Key."

Martí made three more trips to Key West—July 1892, May 1893, and December 1893. He also found financial support for the Cuban cause in Key West's Jewish community. According to one account, "Every Sunday, in Key West, the Jews outfitted a donkey with basket panniers and led it through the streets. Donations to the Cuban cause were put into the baskets." Louis Fine, who lived at 1121 Duval Street next door to cigar manufacturer Teodoro Pérez, helped solicit funds from the Jews in Key West. Fine was chairman of the Committee to Aid the Cubans.

Just how the Cubans themselves were able to contribute so much is due in large part to the institution of the Junta. It is described by war correspondent Trumbull White:

> The Junta is the organization through which Cuba's friends reach the Cubans in the field. In the United States and Europe there are 300 Cuban revolutionary clubs, with a

José Martí, leader of the Cuban revolution, poses on the balcony of 1125 Duval Street (today's La-Te-Da). Martí is standing second from the right with a small girl in front of him. The photograph was taken during his fund-raising visit to Key West in May 1893 when a rally was held at the home of Teodoro Pérez, secretary of the Cigar Manufacturers Union.

membership of more than 50,000. These clubs were the outcome of a suggestion originating with José Martí, and their organization has been accomplished by the delegation, with whom they are all in closest touch, to whom they all account, and through whom they all make contributions in money, clothing, provisions, arms, and munitions for those who are enduring the hardships of the war....

It has further been the business of the Junta—attended by risk of life to its agents—to keep in communication with the insurgents. This has been done by secret agents who come and go from New York to Key West, from Key West to Havana, from Havana into Spanish cities of Cuba and through the provinces of the island.

The cigar makers of Key West, Tampa, Jacksonville, New

York and other cities where large colonies have congregated, have proven their patriotism and their adherences to the cause by giving more generously of their earnings than has ever been done before by the people of any country struggling for freedom. There is scarcely an exception to the assertion that every Cuban in America has shared in contributions to the war fund.

The minimum contribution has been ten per cent of the weekly earnings, and this has brought an enormous sum into the coffers of the Junta for war purposes.

On March 9, 1893, Martí wrote to four wealthy Key West businessmen—Eduardo Gato, Carlos Recio, Manuel Barranco, and Teodoro Pérez—members of the Cayo Hueso Club. Martí needed $12,000 to $14,000 immediately, and $35,000 later for the revolutionary movement. Nine days later he asked the Key West community for $59,000 within a month—two-thirds of what he expected from all the emigre colonies. "The emigre colonies will come through, and the Key [Martí's affectionate name for Key West] will be the first [to come through] with its part of the sacred sum, in spite of shortages and alarms about business," Martí wrote.

The "alarms about business" throughout the United States were very real in the spring of 1893. A move to use silver to back U.S. currency triggered a run on the gold supply. Called the Panic of 1893, this led into a recession. Unemployment hit an estimated 2.5 million by the end of the year and cigar sales plummeted. Workers accused the cigar manufacturers of taking advantage of the recession to reduce wages, and they went on strike. Some manufacturers imported Spanish workers from Cuba to replace them. According to one account, Havana papers" bristled with advertisements about free transportation to Key West, proper protection once there, guarantees of good living conditions and the highest rate of pay ever earned by cigar makers."

Worried about the strike and sagging economy, some of Key West's leading citizens formed a committee to recruit Spanish cigar makers. George W. Allen, Judge L. W. Bethel, William H. Williams.

Carlos Recio fled Camaguey province in Cuba after the Ten Years War and settled in Key West where he became a prosperous wholesale grocer. Marti often turned to Recio for money to support the revolution.

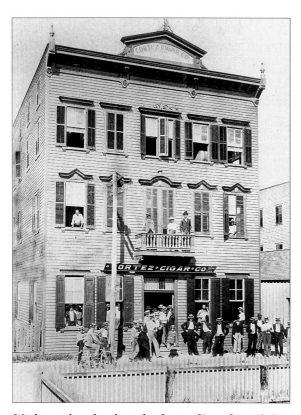

Workers take a break at the Cortez Cigar Co., 113 Ann St. A good cigar-maker could earn from $15 to $30 a week, and many contributed ten percent of that to the Cuban liberation cause. They also paid their readers 25 cents a week. Readers kept the workers entertained and informed by reading from books and newspapers and by passing on the latest news from Cuba.

County Judge A. J. Kemp, W. R. Kerr, the Rev. Charles W. Frazer, and federal marshal John F. Horr were members of the committee that went to Havana and began recruiting Spaniards. The first group of Spanish cigar makers arrived in December 1893. Local Cubans were outraged by the move.

Martí quickly responded by hiring New York attorney Horatio S. Rubens to bring legal action to force the Spanish cigar makers to go back to Cuba.

Rubens charged local federal officials with abetting in the violation of contract labor laws. Finally, after much legal footwork, Washington instructed local U.S. immigration inspectors to arrest the 94 Spaniards and they were eventually returned to Cuba. Jefferson B. Browne, Key West historian, commented, "A spirit of unrest took possession of the Cuban population, who considered the actions of the [committee] unfriendly to them."

Meanwhile Tampa officials, by offering inducements of land and tax breaks, enticed some of the cigar manufacturers to relocate to Tampa. O'Halloran & Co., M. Barranco & Co.., S. & F. Fleitas, Severo de Armas, A. Zamora, and Teodoro Pérez were among those moving to Tampa. Key West's population dropped to an estimated 15,000 in a two year period following the 1893 strike. As wages and population dropped, so did contributions to the revolutionary coffers.

This state of affairs did not stop the revolution. In April 1895, José Martí and General Máximo Gómez led an invasion force on the eastern end of Cuba It was the first major revolution following the Ten Years War and it ended tragically. A Spanish force of over 20,000 met the Cubans May 19, 1895, and Martí was killed. Although Martí's death was a setback, it helped unify the Cuban cause and heighten world interest in the revolution.

Cuban Revolutionary Party headquarters occupied this masonry building which once stood at Whitehead and Caroline Streets, where today's Presidential Gates are located. The Cuban coat-of-arms can be seen on the corner of the building just above the ground floor entrance.

The battleship Maine, *faintly visible in the distance, glides by Fort Taylor. The large mound to the right of center of the fort is a mining casement designed for use in the detonating of mines in the harbor. The* Maine *visited Key West in the summer of 1896 and the winter of 1897.*

The 318-foot battleship Maine *prepares to get underway. The coal-burning ship was built at a cost of $2,500,000. She was commissioned September 17, 1895, and could cut through the water at over 17 knots.*

III

THE BATTLESHIP

In June of 1896 the battleship *Maine* made her first visit to Key West. As a ship of the North Atlantic Squadron she was on a routine tour of duty as a military presence and filibuster deterrent at Key West. During her 52-day stay the *Maine* also provided invaluable aid to local citizens, for while she was here there was a small pox epidemic.

A building had been erected to "quarantine both white and colored with disease," but the city council refused to order all contagious citizens to the building. Dr. Joseph Y. Porter, Florida's first public health officer and a native of Key West, gave the city 12 hours to comply or the entire city would be quarantined. When the council refused, Key West was placed under quarantine from rest of state.

Dr. Porter and a doctor with the U.S. Marine Hospital Service had begun vaccinating adults and children of both races when the *Maine's* captain reported to him upon orders of the Secretary of Navy, offering assistance with the quarantine. Dr. Porter asked the captain to prevent any vessel from entering or leaving Key West without signed authorization. Porter later described what happened:

> Now comes the incident which I wish to stress and how the battleship *Maine* acting as a quarantine steamer, enforced discipline and supported the authority of the State Board of Health of Florida. A wrecking tug put forth to assist the steamer [aground on the reef]. The tug was owned and commanded by one of the 'irreconcilables' who 'would show whether the State Board of Health could interfere with him in his business.' The tug was hailed and called to stop by the officer in the launch, but paid no attention. Evidently from the deck of the *Maine* the maneuvering had been watched and when it was seen that the tug was getting away from the patrol launch, 'boom' went a blank shot from the

Maine, and again no attention was paid to this warning, another shot was fired but this with shotted shell, which fell just in front of the bow of the tug. Result—an immediate turning around of the tug with several of the sail satellites [small sailboats used to ferry arms and men to the filibusters] which had escaped inspection, and a return to the harbor; with likewise an immediate flooding of the State Health Officers's office for vaccination and permits.

A battleship thus acting as a quarantine vessel, and her commanding officer, a man of high rank, under the direction of the Secretary of the Navy enforcing sanitary instructions of the Florida State Board of Health, is, I think, the first instance of the kind in the history of maritime quarantine.

Although Porter in his later years reminiscenced that the officer was Captain Charles D. Sigsbee, the commanding officer of the *Maine* at the time of the quarantine incident was Captain A. S. Crowninshield who was given the ship's first command upon her commissioning in 1895. Porter had confused the first visit of the *Maine* in June 1896 with a later visit of the *Maine* on December 15, 1897 when she returned under the command of Captain Charles D. Sigsbee.

Sigsbee had been to Key West once before in 1878 when he commanded the Coast Survey steamer *Blake*. When he later wrote of the *Maine's* 1897 visit, he noted great changes had occurred in 19 years:

> In the meantime the city had grown and had polished itself amazingly. Formerly orders to Key West were regarded as nearly equivalent to confinement to the ship. The place had no attraction in itself, and there was hardly any exchange of courtesies beween the residents and the naval officers. The market offered little but fish and turtle. But during the *Maine's* visit we had a most agreeable time, and made the acquaintance of many people. The city had decidedly 'gone into society.' Young naval officers were beginning to marry there, and with good reason, according to my view of the matrimonial market.

The *Maine* was kept busy chasing after filibusters running guns and men to Cuba. Captain Sigsbee recalled that at one time there were "five vessels out looking for filibusters and all were in contact with the *Maine* by telegraph—we did our work conscientiously."

The *Maine* spent the Christmas holidays in 1897 anchored in Key West harbor. In his memoirs, Captain Sigsbee cited a local newspaper description of the *Maine's* Christmas display: "The beautiful illumination of the battleship *Maine*, on Christmas eve and night, was one of the finest displays of electricity ever witnessed in the city, or perhaps in the South. Hundreds of incandescent lights from the bow to the stern, up the masts and funnel, and around the ship's sides, made her one mass of lights. It was a picture not often seen in the tropical regions."

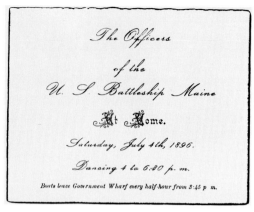

On the **Maine's** *first visit to Key West in the summer of 1896, officers and crew quickly became friends with the townspeople. For the Fourth of July, the officers sent out invitations for a dance aboard ship.*

Seamen of the *Maine* had less enthusiastic memories of a cold Christmas spent at Key West. According to diary entries by Apprentice First Class Ambrose Ham, the men had "no extra dinners. . . . One day we wore overcoats and it is a strange thing to wear overcoats in Key West." After the cold snap passed, however, the crew did enjoy swimming and baseball, and the *Maine's* baseball team was playing late afternoon on January 12 when Captain Sigsbee received a coded message from the American Consul in Havana, General Fitzhugh Lee.

A riot had broken out in Havana and several newspaper offices had been attacked. It was apparently led by Spanish army officers and it was unclear as to whether Americans living in Cuba were in danger. Not wanting to take chances, Lee sent a message to Sigsbee to prepare the *Maine* to get underway. Sigsbee ordered a gun fired—a prearranged signal for all *Maine* men to

Captain Charles D. Sigsbee, stands on the deck the Maine. Sigsbee wrote "At Key West I both accepted and gave a few luncheons or dinners. People from ashore appeared to enjoy shipboard entertainments beyond reason as conceived by those who entertain afloat; novelty garnishes the feast, I suppose."

The Maine's baseball team played ball with some of the local teams during their Key West visit the winter of 1897. The team's mascot, a goat, stayed behind in Key West when the Maine left to go to Havana. When the Maine sank, Landsman John H. Bloomer of East Deering, Maine (back row, far left) was the only member of team who survived.

In 1969 when he was 84 years old, former Monroe County Sheriff Berlin Sawyer recalled selling homemade candy and newspapers aboard the *Maine* and other ships:

"We were real poor. I went out to work when I was 10 years old to help my mother. I used to go down to the wharf and get on the barge and go out to the battleship *Maine* and sell a lot of stuff to the men on the ship.

"The cook always gave me back the paper I sold him so I could sell it again. And he used to give me a hearty meal of whatever he was cooking up for the crew. . . . It was the one real good meal I got each day cause we were living on grits at home."

He recalled that the evening the *Maine* pulled up anchor to leave Key West, he was still aboard. Although one of the officers told him he could stay aboard until the ship got back, Sawyer said he realized his mother would be worried. He ran down to deck to Captain Sigsbee's quarters, but the guard would not let him pass.

"But I just waited 'til he had his back turned and dashed right into Captain Sigsbee's cabin." Captain Sigsbee knew of Sawyer's providing for the family and ordered a boat launched to return the lad to shore. "That was the *Maine's* last visit before she sank in Havana harbor—and I might have been on board."

return aboard—and the baseball game was called. Later, while awaiting the word from Lee to leave Key West, Sigsbee and several of his officers went ashore to a dance to divert the suspicion of correspondents. "I was asked a number of questions about the departure of the *Maine*," Sigsbee said later of this alert, "but we managed so well that some of the crew had already given out that we were going to New York."

It was a case of "hurry up and wait." The *Maine* would stay at Key West for nearly two more weeks before receiving orders to go to Havana.

Meanwhile, the squadron had been ordered to go to Key West. On January 23 the ships anchored near Sand Key—the largest gathering of United States naval vessels since the Civil War.

Because of the size of the fleet and its demands for coal, the ships were to go to the fleet anchorage at Dry Tortugas. The *Maine* received orders to join the squadron at the Tortugas, and on January 24 left Key West for the last time.

After arriving at the Tortugas anchorage that night, Sigsbee went on board the battleship *New York*. Here he was given orders to proceed to Havana and "make friendly call—Pay [your] respects to authorities there—Particular attention must be paid to usual interchange of civility." Returning to his ship, Sigsbee ordered the *Maine* underway.

Making her way slowly so as to arrive in full daylight, the battleship *Maine* arrived in Havana Harbor at 10:00 A.M. on January 25.

Coaling the ships of the fleet was a mammoth task. Coal was shipped to Key West, unloaded and stored in sheds near the waterfront. Manual labor and mule-power were used to move the coal from the sheds to the docks, where it was then shoveled into those ships whose draft allowed them to dock there. Deeper draft vessels had to be coaled offshore, or at the Dry Tortugas.

The Maine *exploded in Havana Harbor the night of February 15, 1898. Red Cross founder Clara Barton was in Havana at the time and wrote: "The air was filled with a blaze of light, and this in turn filled with black specks like huge specters flying in all directions." The painting is by W. Louis Sonntag.*

```
SECNAV--WASHINGTON, D.C. MAINE BLOWN UP IN HAVANA HARBOR
AT NINE FORTY TONIGHT AND DESTROYED. MANY WOUNDED AND
DOUBTLESS MORE KILLED OR DROWNED. WOUNDED AND OTHERS ON
BOARD SPANISH MAN-OF-WAR AND WARD LINE STEAMER. SEND LIGHT
HOUSE TENDERS FROM KEY WEST FOR CREW AND THE FEW PIECES OF
EQUIPMENT ABOVE WATER. NO ONE HAS CLOTHING OTHER THAN
UPON HIM. PUBLIC OPINION SHOULD BE SUSPENDED UNTIL FURTHER
REPORT. ALL OFFICERS BELIEVED TO BE SAVED. JENKINS AND
MERRITT NOT YET ACCOUNTED FOR. MANY SPANISH OFFICERS,
INCLUDING REPRESENTATIVES OF GENERAL BLANCO, NOW WITH ME
TO EXPRESS SYMPATHY.
```

Telegram sent by Captain Sigsbee to Secretary of Navy John D. Long two hours after battleship **Maine** *blew up February 15, 1898. Lt. F. W. Jenkins and assistant engineer D. R. Merritt were both killed.*

IV

An Explosion in Havana Harbor

For 21 days the *Maine* lay anchored in Havana harbor, its crew confined to ship, and the ship kept under steam in order to be prepared for any eventuality. Although Sigsbee and his officers entertained Americans and Cubans on board the *Maine*, visited Spanish authorities, and even attended a bull fight, it was all done very cautiously.

Despite the tension, the days settled into tedious routine and time passed uneventfully—until the night of February 15, 1898. At 9:40 P.M. the battleship *Maine* exploded and sank. Of the 355 men she carried, only 94 would survive. The explosion was a shocking surprise.

Of all the world, Key West heard the news first. Domingo Villaverde, a Cuban telegraph operator in the Havana office of the International Ocean Telegraph Company, asked Thomas K. Warren, the Key West operator, to turn off the wire going north from Key West because he wanted to relay a personal message. Warren obliged and the first news of the *Maine* exploding was received in the Key West office at Greene Street and Telegraph Lane.

Villaverde's short message told of hearing a terrific explosion and seeing smoke rise from where the *Maine* had been anchored. Warren, realizing the seriousness of the message, notified his boss, Martin L. Hellings. Unbeknownst to Warren, Hellings had been doing intelligence work for months for the U.S. government. As manager of the Key West office, he worked with Villaverde to establish an intelligence network between Cuba, Key West, and Washington, D.C. Thanks to their efforts, copies of top-secret Spanish material were sent directly to the White House—at the same time they were being sent to Spain. According to author G. J. A. O'Toole, "Nothing happened in Cuba that President McKinley did not know of within an hour."

Hellings immediately contacted his local navy intelligence liaison, Lieutenant Albert Gleaves, commander of torpedo boat *Cushing*. Gleaves and Lt. Commander W. S. Cowles came to the telegraph office

A group of telegraph company employees and friends pose in front of the office of International Ocean Telegraph Company at Greene Street and Telegraph Alley. Communications with Cuba were carried over the submerged cable which had been laid between Key West and Havana in 1867. The building houses retail shops today.

to wait for official confirmation, which would arrive two hours later.

In Havana, Captain Sigsbee had survived the explosion and with members of the crew made his way in the captain's gig to the Ward Line steamer *City of Washington*, a passenger ship anchored nearby. Here he got George Bronson Rea, correspondent for *Harper's Weekly*, to take two messages ashore for transmittal. One was sent to Secretary of the Navy John D. Long in Washington and the other to Commander James M. Forsyth, commandant of the Key West Naval Station. The Key West message read "Tell admiral *Maine* blown up and destroyed. Send light-house tenders. Many killed and wounded. Don't send war vessels if others available." Forsyth immediately dispatched the lighthouse tender *Mangrove* to Havana at 3 A.M. Wednesday.

The Convent of Mary Immaculate was

P. L. Cosgrove, Sr., was captain of the lighthouse tender **Mangrove**, *the first rescue ship sent from Key West to Havana after the* **Maine** *exploded.*

completing commencement exercises in the auditorium of the new San Carlos Institute on Duval Street when cries of "*Maine* Blown Up!" were heard. Years later, Sister M. Louis Gabriel would recall that the graduates and audience were so upset that she had to call a policeman to reassure and calm the people.

All over Key West the tumultuous news was greeted with alarm, and in some cases, enthusiasm. Local men, anxious to jump into whatever fray developed, sent the following telegram to Florida Governor William D. Bloxham: "Key West Volunteer Artillery Ready—Fifty Men." It was 9:06 A.M. February 16—less than 12 hours after the *Maine* sank. Throughout the country, reaction was much the same. People were shocked and angry, and most blamed the explosion on Spain—led in their reactions by the sensational reporting in the American press.

The morning after the *Maine's* explosion, the Reverend Mother Mary Florentine, Superior of the Convent of Mary Immaculate, sent word to Commander Forsyth offering the use of the Convent buildings and the services of some 20 nuns as nurses. The Sisters had helped the community before by serving as nurses during small pox and yellow fever outbreaks.

Around midnight February 16 the steamship *Olivette* arrived with some of the wounded. One was Seaman Ambrose Ham who

The Plant Line steamer **Olivette** *brought sailors who survived the* **Maine***'s explosion to Key West and Tampa. On the return trip, the* **Olivette** *carried Navy divers to recover bodies and gather information to help the Court of Inquiry.*

William Randolph Hearst and other newspaper publishers helped push the United States into war with their "yellow journalism" coverage of events in Cuba. His pro-war report in the New York Journal February 17, 1898, quoted Assistant Secretary of the Navy Theodore Roosevelt as the source that the explosion was no accident.

wrote that despite the lateness of the hour they were greeted by a large crowd of citizens. "Some [of us] were taken to the Marine Hospital," Ham wrote, "But I went to the Army Hospital. We had nice beds to sleep in and good food. The stewards and nurses did all in their power to help. Almost every day we received fruit and cake from some kind-hearted lady." One seaman from the *Maine* was already in Key West. Left behind when the *Maine* left for Havana was Martin Larsen who was suffering from a bad fever. He was still in the Marine Hospital when the wounded from the *Maine* started arriving.

Flags were ordered flown at half-mast in memory of the *Maine*, and on February 19, Rear Admiral Montgomery Sicard, Commander-in-Chief U.S. Naval Force on North Atlantic Station, ordered a Court of Inquiry to find out what caused the explosion. The Court convened for the first time February 21 aboard the lighthouse tender *Mangrove* in Havana Harbor.

A nurse at the Marine Hospital bandages a wounded soldier in this illustration entitled "An Angel of Mercy." Ft. Taylor appears in the distance through the open window.

Captain Sigsbee escorts a boatload of coffins with the remains of his men recovered from the Maine *in the right background. Some coffins were brought to Key West where the men were buried in the local cemetery.*

The four man court was headed by Captain William T. Sampson, president; Captain French E. Chadwick; Lt. Commander William P. Potter; and Lt. Commander Adolph Marix, judge advocate. Marix was a former executive officer of the *Maine*. He had been transferred to another ship before the *Maine* left Norfolk in December 1897.

The same day the Court of Inquiry convened in Havana, inspection of the coal piles began in Key West. Spontaneous combustion of the coal was a distinct possibility, for many coal bunker fires had previously been reported on U.S. Navy ships—including one the afternoon of December 10, 1895 on the cruiser *Cincinnati* in Key West harbor. According to the *Cincinnati's* captain, "Spontaneous combustion in the coal bunkers went undiscovered until the fire reached the magazine, and smoke

Wounded from the Maine *were treated in the Marine Hospital. The building was designed by Robert Mills, architect of the Washington Monument and built in 1844 with federal funding for benefit of sick and injured seamen. Called Mills Place today, it is the oldest building on the former naval station.*

was seen coming from burning boxes containing ammunition. The forward magazine was flooded and the fire put out." Key West historian Jefferson Browne speculated that "had it been at night as in the case of the *Maine*, the smoke would not likely have been seen, and the tragedy of the *Maine* in Havana harbor would have had a forerunner on the *Cincinnati* in the harbor of Key West"

Entries in the commandant's log of Key West Naval Station for three days record the tedious work: February 21—"Commenced to examining the anthracite coal piles—carefully, moving it over with shovels under the close personal observation of [a four man crew];" February 22—"Inspection of anthracite coal piles continues;" February 23—"Finished overhauling [the] anthracite coat piles found no signs of anything suspicious." Commander Forsyth would later tell the court that the men inspecting the coal "examined it lump by lump" and found nothing suspicious.

The Court of Inquiry finished its investigation in Havana, and moved to Key West on February 28—the same day the steamer *Bache* arrived with first body to be buried in what would later become the *Maine* plot in the Key West cemetery. Ten days earlier the *Bache* had taken a team of Navy divers to Havana to begin the recovery of bodies. Although some were buried in Havana, after February 28 all bodies would be brought to Key West.

In Key West, the Court of Inquiry met on the second floor of the

Reverend Gilbert Higgs, rector of St. Paul's Episcopal Church, conducts funeral services in the Key West City Cemetery. A Navy honor guard stands ready to fire a salute over flag-draped coffins of the men from the **Maine.**

On the second floor of the red brick Custom House, the Court of Inquiry met to interview sailors from the **Maine** *and divers who had surveyed the wreckage of the ship. The building was completed in 1891 and housed the post office, the lighthouse board, and the federal court.*

Custom House at Clinton Place. Shortly after noon on March 2, Judge Advocate Marix told the court that they had interviewed all of the survivors of the *Maine* except the wounded.

To interview them, the court went to the U.S. Army Barracks Hospital where all the survivors of the *Maine* who were able to get out of bed were assembled. After being sworn in as a group, the sailors were asked if anyone knew of any negligence on part of the crew to step forward. No one did and the court finished its inquiry.

Twenty-three days after it began, the Court of Inquiry concluded that the *Maine* was destroyed by a submarine mine which had blown up several compartments where ammunition was stored. The court, however, could not determine who was responsible for the explosion. The Spanish, who had started their own investigation the day after the explosion, had concluded the opposite—that the cause of the explosion must have been internal.

Over 75 years later, Admiral Hyman G. Rickover, head of the U.S. naval nuclear propulsion program, became intrigued about the unresolved cause of the explosion. He put together a team of structural and chemical engineers, a historian, and a museum curator to review the findings of the American and Spanish courts of inquiry and those of a later investigation made when the *Maine* was raised in 1911-12.

After reviewing all of the evidence, Rickover's team concluded:

> We have found no technical evidence in the records examined that an external explosion initiated the destruction of the *Maine*. The available evidence is consistent with an internal explosion alone. We therefore conclude that an internal source was the cause of the explosion. The most likely source was heat from a fire in the coal bunker adjacent to the 6-inch reserve magazine. However, since there is no way of proving this, other internal causes cannot be eliminated as possibilities.

Court of Inquiry into the sinking of the **Maine** *convenes on the second floor of the Custom House in Key West. From left to right are: Captain French E. Chadwick, president; Captain William T. Sampson, Lieutenant Commander William P. Potter, an unidentified civilian standing, an unidentified civilian sitting, and seated in the foreground, Lieutenant Commander Adolph Marix.*

V

WAITING FOR WAR

"Remember the *Maine*!" became the rallying cry of the nation, and Key West became the recipient for outpourings of grief and sympathy. Typical of the reaction nationwide was that of Mrs. William Swain of Philadelphia who sent a $20 bill to Commander Forsyth in Key West "to be used in the purchase of cigars and other luxuries for the wounded sailors of the ill-fated *Maine*." According to the *Florida Times-Union* March 25, 1898, there were 13 wounded men of the *Maine* in the hospitals of Key West, 11 in the U.S. Army Barracks Hospital and two in the Marine Hospital.

Ships of the North Atlantic Fleet and others were ordered to Key West, including the "mightiest warship afloat," the first-class battleship *Oregon*, which left California on March 19. By March 25 the torpedo boat *Winslow* had arrived from Norfolk and joined 39 other war vessels off Key West.

Such an staggering increase in the fleet impacted the city in many ways. Work began on enlarging the large coal warehouse on Philbrick's wharf at the end of Duval Street to double its former capacity, and the Navy pushed construction of large coal storehouses on a vacant lot just south of the Custom House. Purchased by the Navy in 1895, this prime waterfront property was where Mrs. Ellen

Troops sent to Key West were often quartered in tents set up on the grounds of the army barracks (today's Peary Court). Artist Frederic Remington sketched these scenes of soldiers cooking and standing guard duty.

Mallory, mother of the Confederate Secretary of Navy Stephen R. Mallory, once operated "The Coconut Grove," a boarding house.

By the end of March, the United States government had rented every vacant storehouse in the lower part of the city to store provisions which were arriving daily. Moving the tremendous flow of supplies and people strained the public transportation system of hacks and mule-powered streetcars. In early April, H. L. Stricker, president of Philbrick's Electric Light and Street Railway (a predecessor of today's City Electric System), announced that within a very few weeks electric streetcars would be running over at least one line. The company also expected to have its new ice plant in operation about the same time.

In the midst of all the hustle and bustle of military buildup, the city was dealing with the survivors, the bodies, and the wreckage of the battleship *Maine*.

On March 16, Commander Forsyth issued an order to have additional graves dug by the side of the ten already filled with victims of the *Maine*. The steamer *Olivette*, which had been shuttling between Key West and Havana, brought five or six more unidentified bodies that day. In a procedure that was becoming all too familiar, the *Olivette* was met by naval officials and funeral director B. P. Baker, and burial took place immediately.

Civilians help unload military supplies at the government wharf behind the Naval Depot (today's Clinton Market). The tons of supplies which flooded Key West in anticipation of war were stored in all available warehouses, and more had to be built along the waterfront.

Baker, a dealer in furniture and building materials located on Simonton Street between Front and Greene, advertised "Undertaking in all its branches attended to with promptness and in the best manner." His service was later recognized by Commander Forsyth who chose Baker to be grand marshal of the parade when the monument to the *Maine* victims was dedicated in the city cemetery.

Throughout March, more bodies from the *Maine* were buried. City marshal Richard T. Hicks was praised for keeping the funeral processions "free of noisy and obnoxious characters" during processions to the cemetery. The city aldermen added six police officers to the force because of so much activity and excitement.

Benjamin P. Baker was the prominent local businessman, cabinet-maker, and undertaker who handled the burial arrangements for the dead brought to Key West.

The arrival of a ship carrying bodies from the *Maine* toward the end of March also brought wreckage from the battleship. This attracted souvenir hunters from all over, anxious to get a piece of the *Maine*. Metal salvaged from the historic ship was later made into souvenir spoons, plaques, coins, watch cases, and plates.

The first motion pictures ever taken in Key West were made on March 27. Photographer William Paley arrived in time to film *Burial of the* Maine *Victims*. This 150-foot-long film showed a procession of nine hearses, each draped with an American flag. Other motion picture sequences taken in Key West included one showing the monitor *Terror* coaling at the government wharf, and *War Correspondents*, a staged scene in which journalists raced to the cable office to telegraph news to their newspapers.

Stuck in Key West, waiting for war to be declared, the correspondents published their own news sheet called the *Scorpion*. According to historian Marie Cappick, writers from throughout the world who were covering the war were the contributors to its columns. Copies of this paper and also the *Key West Herald* have apparently not survived.

The *Key West Herald* was the local newspaper for the English-speaking citizens of the island and it was kept busy during this period. The demand for news of activity around the island and developments in Washington became so intense that some days the *Herald* had to issue multiple editions.

El Yara, the local Spanish language newspaper, was the "official organ of several Cuban Revolutionary Clubs of Key West, Florida." Published daily, it was read faithfully by the patriots in Key West. It was also sent to supporters in Tampa and New York, and to the revolutionary soldiers in Cuba. José Dolores Poyo, the editor, was a close friend of Marti. A few scattered copies of *El Yara* exist.

The U.S. Navy continued to prepare its ships for war by stripping them of all unneeded woodwork, removing the small boats, and painting them. The color of the paint became an issue. The first order was to paint the ships black, but someone realized this color only made them stand out, and an order came down to stop the painting. Captain William T. Sampson recommended the now familiar battleship gray. Fortunately when the order to stop painting the ships was issued, only two had been completely painted black.

Activity continued to intensify on the military front when Florida Governor William D. Bloxham ordered Captain F. C. Brossier to put the Key West Guards (similar to the National Guard today) on a war footing to be in readiness to move at any time.

The government was also readying Key West coastal defenses against possible attack by Spanish forces. The harbor was mined in early April by a detachment from the United States marine engineer battalion at Wilmette Point, N. Y. The mines could be detonated from a control bunker located near Ft. Taylor.

Work had begun before the *Maine's* explosion on modernizing Ft. Taylor by cutting off the top tier to reduce the profile of the fort and make it less of a target because weapons had improved vastly since the Civil War. In March, work began on Batteries Osceola and Adair at the fort. Osceola housed two modern 12-inch rifles and Adair held four 3-

Fort Taylor was still surrounded by water at the time of the Spanish-American War, but work had already been started on removing the top tier of the casemates, or gunrooms. This detail is from a 1870s painting by Seth Eastman.

inch, 18-pounder rapid-fire rifles. They were built with labor imported from Jacksonville, Mobile, and other Gulf ports. The navy, pressed for storage, was allowed to store ammunition at the fort.

At Ft. Jefferson in the Dry Tortugas, the navy dredged the channels deeper and began expanding the coaling station to hold 20,000 tons of coal so that the largest and deepest draft battleships could be coaled right at the docks. The expansion, however, was not completed until three years later. The Secretary of the Navy reported that "had the war with Spain continued many months more, the absence of docking facilities in these waters would have been most seriously felt and the failure to possess such might, in a more prolonged war, seriously affect its fortunes."

A "home guard" was organized by Dr. Jeptha Vining Harris for the defense of the city. Harris had served as a doctor for the Confederacy during the Civil War and had moved to Key West in the 1870s. Here he established a medical practice and became active in Democratic politics. "As usual Dr. Harris appears to have struck the popular chord, therefore, he will have no trouble in raising a full company," the *Florida Times-Union* noted. It reported that "Fighting Jeptha's Home Guard" had already been joined by the following men: J. Melinhan, J. Markowitz, J. Renbin, Isidor Roberts, E. Baker, A. Page, W. Ridlon, A. Taylor, C. Roberts, T. Sweeting, W. G. Gorden.

The Key West Guard is shown at their Tallahassee encampment in May 1897. Benjamin D. Jenks, standing third from left, worked for the local newspaper and was the correspondent for the Florida Times-Union. *Copies of his dispatches provide the most significant local history of the era since the local newspapers have not survived. Other members in the photograph are left to right, standing: Leon Roberts, A. C. Jenks, B. D. Jenks, Charles O'Brien, Willie Gandolfo; seated: H. D. Herrick, John Navarro, Mot Curry.*

Meanwhile, Americans living in Cuba began to leave in great numbers. On April 6, the Plant Line steamer *Mascotte* arrived with 96 Americans who were anxious to leave Havana before war broke out. As soon as the ship had unloaded the passengers and freight, she coaled at the government dock and returned to Havana for more

The Mascotte *leaves Havana Harbor under the guns of Morro Castle. On April 7, the* Mascotte *brought over more than 700 Americans and another 200 Cuban refugees. The U.S. government paid the Peninsular and Occidental Steamship Company $15,000 for providing this emergency transportation.*

The Key West Cornet Band leads a joyful procession of Cubans and Key Westers in celebrating the Congressional declaration of a "free Cuba" April 20. The happy demonstrators are shown marching in front of the Custom House at Clinton Place. Two days later the North Atlantic Squadron left to blockade Cuba.

fleeing Americans. Some of the arriving passengers, concerned over the proximity of Key West to Cuba, took the Peninsular and Occidental Steamship Company's *City of Key West* to Miami and points north as soon as they could.

In Washington, the situation was rapidly moving to a head. On April 20, President McKinley signed a joint resolution passed by Congress "for the recognition of the independence of the people of Cuba, demanding that the government of Spain relinquish its authority and government in the island of Cuba and Cuban waters." The resolution directed the President "to use the land and naval forces of the United States to carry these resolutions into effect."

On April 22, the North Atlantic fleet left Tortugas to go to Cuba to blockade the island. That same day the Sister Superior assembled the 600 students of the Convent and told them that classes would be suspended until after the war, for the navy had officially accepted her offer of the Convent for a hospital. "When will we return to our dear Convent?" one student asked. No one knew.

Sister Louis Gabriel later recalled that the nuns had to empty the school of desks, chairs and furnishings, reserving the chapel, community room, two dormitories, a dining room, and laundry for their use. "Two by two we went out," she said, "searching all day long for vacant warehouses, empty cigar factories. By nightfall, we had found enough. The next day, with mules and carts and drivers, we emptied the place and scrubbed it. When the doctors came back they were amazed at what had been done in two days." Major W. R. Hall, physician in charge of the hospital, said "Mother Florentine, in this convent you may be called Mother Superior, but you are really a general of the Army."

Reverend Mother Mary Florentine was Superior of the Convent of Mary Immaculate during the Spanish-American War.

VI

THE FIRST SHOT

On April 21, a few miles off Key West, Captain William T. Sampson received word he had just been promoted to rear admiral with "command of the U.S. forces on the North Atlantic station." That evening he summoned the commanding officers of the fleet to his flagship, the *New York*. Samspon gave the officers their orders by reading a telegram from President McKinley: "War declared; proceed to blockade the coast of Cuba."

Richard Harding Davis described the events that followed in his book, *The Cuban and Porto Rican Campaigns*:

> There were still ships to coal, or Captain Sampson, who had become Admiral Sampson since half-past four, would on the word have started to blockade Havana. But as they could not be left behind, all of those ships that were ready were moved outside the harbor and the fleet was signaled to be in readiness to start at four o'clock—the next morning. That night as the sunk sank—and it sinks at Key West with a splendor and glory that it assumes in but few other ports in the world—it spread a fiery red background for thirteen black ships of war outlined with gallows-like yards against the sky. Some still lay at anchor, sparkling with cargo lights and with the coaling barges looming bulkily along side, and others moved across the crimson curtain looking less like ships than a procession of grotesque monsters of the sea—grim, inscrutable, and menacing. . . .
>
> And yet while men wondered as to what the morrow might bring forth, the physical aspect of the night was one in strange contrast to the great change of the day. We could imagine the interest and excitement which the declaration of war had roused in all corners of the country: we knew that

for the moment Key West was the storm-centre of the map of the United States, and that where the squadron would go, what it would do, and how soon it would move upon the enemy were questions that men were asking in clubs and on street corners; we knew that bulletin-boards were blocking the streets of lower New York with people eager for news, and that men and women from Seattle to Boston were awake with anxiety and unrest.

And yet at the heart of it all, in the harbor of Key West, save for the water lapping against the great sides of the ships and the bells sounding in chorus across the stretches of the bay, there was only silence, and the night wore every aspect of peace. For though all through that night the vessels talked with one another, they spoke in languages of signs—a language that made less sound than a whisper. That was the only promise for the morrow, their rows of lanterns winking red and white against the night, and vanishing instantly in mid-air, and the great fingers of the search-lights sweeping grandly across the sky, halting upright for a moment, and

"With our fleet at Key West—torpedo boat Cushing *carrying dispatches to the Flag-Ship,*" *was the caption for this sketch that appeared in* Harper's Weekly *on April 23, 1898; "The* New York, Indiana, *and* Iowa *are lying ten miles out in the Gulf, where the sea runs high in the strong trade-wind." The artist was Carlton T. Chapman.*

then sinking to the water's edge, measuring out the heavens and carrying messages of command to men many miles at sea.

The morning of the [22nd] awoke radiantly beautiful with light and color. In the hollows of the waves deep blue and purple shadows caught the million flashes of the sun, and their white crests danced in its light. Across this flashing picture of movement and color, the leaden-painted warships moved heavily in two great columns, the battleships and monitors leading on the left, the cruisers moving abreast to starboard, while in their wake and on either flank the torpedo-boats rolled and tossed like porpoises at play. To the active imagination it might have appeared that each was racing to be the first to throw a shell into Cabáñas prison, to knock the first stone from the ramparts of Morro Castle, to fire the first shot of the War of '98. But the first shot of the war was reserved for no such serious purpose.

For while the houses of Key West were still well in view, there came into the lines of the squadron a courteous Spaniard, who, unsuspecting and innocent of war, steered his tramp steamer, the *Buena Ventura*, into the very jaws of the enemy. And it was upon him that the unsought-for honor fell of receiving the first shot our navy had fired "in anger" in thirty years.

Richard Harding Davis covered the Spanish-American War for the New York Journal. *He was also correspondent for the* London Times.

Officers and men from the gunboat Nashville *prepare to board the* Buena Ventura, *first prize ship captured in the Spanish-American War. The Spanish steamer was carrying a cargo of lumber and was valued at $150,000. She was the first of many captured ships that would be held at Key West.*

"Five Captured Spanish Vessels Towed into Key West in Three Days" read the caption on this illustration by F. C. Schell in Leslie's Weekly. *The* Buena Ventura *is at far right; Ft. Taylor is at far left. Captains and crews of the prize ships were not allowed to leave them during their stay in Key West.*

Cubans who fled their homeland after the United States formally declared war against Spain arrived at Mallory Square aboard the lighthouse tender **Mangrove**. The refugees walk quickly past the building which today houses the Greater Key West Chamber of Commerce. This scene appeared in **Harper's** Weekly April 30.

Harper's Weekly *published this photograph of "the arrival of the 25th Infantry (Colored) at Key West." The 25th Infantry was a regular army group whose two companies camped in tents along the waterfront near the Custom House, at Ft. Taylor, and on the grounds of the Army Barracks. The troops are shown marching along Front Street near the Fitzpatrick Street entrance to Mallory Square.*

VII

Wartime Key West

The first shot of the Spanish-American War on April 22, 1898, stopped the *Buena Ventura* in her tracks. When the Spanish steamer hove to and a boarding party from the *Nashville* under Ensign T. P. Magruder was put aboard, the astonished captain told Magruder he did not know that war had been declared. The *Nashville* escorted her prize into Key West harbor at 11:00 A.M., setting off a jubilant dockside celebration. It seemed fitting that the Spanish name of the first prize of war translated into "good fortune."

Technically, war had not yet been declared. When the North Atlantic Squadron began the blockade of Cuba within hours of leaving Dry Tortugas on April 22, Spain had responded by saying the blockade was an act of war. President McKinley quickly sent a message to Congress Monday, April 25 asking for a declaration of war. A bill was introduced and passed in the House that declared a state of war existed between Spain and the United States and "had existed since and including April 21." The Senate concurred and the bill promptly became law.

Starting immediately there were many changes. The Spanish Vice Consul and his clerk left Key West, and the office of the Spanish consulate was transferred to the British Consul. The Key West telegraph office was turned over to the United States Signal Service Corps on April 28. Henceforth, every telegram sent out of Key West would pass through a censor.

On May 1, more than 100 Cubans enlisted in Key West to join the revolutionary forces in their homeland, and more signed up in the following days. No roster exists of the Cubans from Key West who joined the insurgents, but relatives have confirmed that Juan Carbonell, José P. Mira, and two sons of José Pérez Coto served in the war. All young and healthy Cubans who were willing to fight were told to go to Tampa by Estrada Palma, junta leader from New York, and 600 Cuban

Cigar manufactuer Juan Carbonell (left), joined with hundreds of Key West Cubans who volunteered for the insurgent forces at the beginning of the war. In later years, Carbonell opened the Monroe and Strand Theatres on Duval Street.

volunteers from all over answered the call. Under the command of Emilio Núñez, general of the Army of the Cuban Republic, they sailed from Port Tampa with 7,000 rifles.

In Key West the ranks of "Fighting Jeptha's Home Guards" were rapidly filling up—it was noted that even a Spaniard had enrolled. Some residents who feared what the war might bring to Key West, however, decided to leave the city. The American schooner *Holly Hock* sailed for Nassau with some Bahamians who were fearful that Spain would capture Key West.

Red Cross founder Clara Barton arrived in Key West Friday April 29 from Tampa on the *Mascotte* with a party of four doctors, a wife of one doctor, four nurses, a financial secretary and two assistants. The group boarded the *State of Texas*, a Red Cross ship, which was scheduled to carry Barton's party and supplies to Cuba. Clearance to leave, however, was not given for weeks. While waiting, Barton recorded in her diary that "all days are

Clara Barton and her party prepare for a sail in Key West harbor. They were waiting permission to go to Cuba to distribute food and clothing to the Cuban people and to provide medical supplies and assistance to the U.S. forces. Barton, founder of the American Red Cross, is the woman in black on the right.

Captured Spanish vessels, prizes of war, are shown anchored in Man-of-War Harbor (near today's Trumbo Point on the U.S. Naval Station) off the end of the U.S. Army Barracks (today's Peary Court). Clara Barton and her staff helped feed the Spaniards who were not permitted ashore. Sketch is by Carlton T. Chapman, "special artist for Harper's Weekly."

clear, fine, sunny and warm . . . there have been no rains since October . . . the wells are dry."

Later she recorded that she had a "very pleasant" time having lunch with the Rev. Charles W. Frazer, pastor of the First Congregational Church. The Red Cross staff also visited the graves of the sailors from the Maine

By mid-May, the Red Cross was feeding the crews of 15-20 Spanish ships, "prizes" captured by the U.S. Navy. Nearly 200 Spaniards, mostly fishermen, could not leave their ships and the U.S. government was not allowed to assist them. The plight of some of the captured seamen was not always so distressing, however. According to one newspaper account, some of the Spanish detained on the captured vessels "live like princes of large inheritance and entertain their guests with all the elaborate politeness and generous hospitality of their race. They give course dinners, have the choicest Spanish wines and cigars, and treat the United States officers who visit them as if they were petted friends instead of dreaded captors."

In Cuba, the blockade continued without serious incident until May 11 when the first fatalities of the war occurred. On the northern coast of Cuba at Cardenas, Spanish gunboats protecting the harbor opened fire as the torpedo boat *Winslow*, revenue cutter *Hudson*, and the cruiser *Wilmington* moved toward them. The *Winslow* took the

Funeral procession for four sailors from the Winslow *heads along Eaton Street to St. Paul's Episcopal Church. Services were held May 12 for the men, who were then buried in the city cemetery. In 1898, St. Paul's was located on Eaton between Duval and Bahama Streets; steeples of the Methodist and Baptist churches are at left.*

brunt of the fire.

Five dead and several wounded men from the torpedo boat were quickly brought to Key West. On May 13, a funeral service for the first fatality of the war, Ensign Worth Bagley, was held at St. Paul's Episcopal Church. After the service, fourteen surviving sailors from the *Winslow* escorted his body to a boat for shipment to North Carolina. The procession was headed by an honor guard of 50 marines and an equal number of bluejackets from the torpedo boats

More elaborate services had been held the day before at St. Paul's and the city cemetery for *Winslow* firemen first class John Dueefe and George Burton Meeks; oiler

"Gallant crew of the torpedo boat Winslow*" is how the photographer described the group who lost five shipmates when the Spanish shelled their boat off the Cuban coast at Cardenas May 11, 1898. Wounded sailors from the* Winslow *were treated at the Convent Hospital and some of the dead were buried in the city cemetery.*

John Varveres, a Greek national; and cook E. J. "Isaia" Tunnell, first black killed during the war.

According to the *Florida Times-Union*, "bareheaded men, women and children lined the entire route of the [funeral procession from the church to the cemetery], and every one of the hundreds of flags in the city was lowered to half-mast." A drummer, a bugler, and 16 Marines from the *Panther* headed the cortege. Over 200 men from the warships in the harbor marched in sections behind the Marines and each hearse. Behind the hearses and escorts followed a long line of carriages containing Navy officers and local citizens.

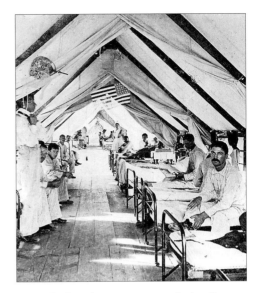

Tents had to be set up around the Convent Hospital to take care of the many men wounded during the battle of Santiago in early July. The hospital began receiving Santiago wounded July 5 and eventually over 300 wounded were cared for from the Santiago battle.

In the cemetery, just behind the graves of the *Maine* sailors, four holes had been dug in the coral rock. The Marine guard lined up on one side of the open graves and as each coffin was lowered, Episcopal rector Gilbert Higgs read the burial service. Finally, the Marines fired three volleys into the air and the bugler sounded taps.

The Convent Hospital, rushed to readiness, had admitted its first patient on May 6. He was not a casualty of war but John H. Speel from Minnesota, paymaster on the *Amphitrite*, who was suffering from "Neurasthenia"—fatigue, "loss of memory and energy."

On May 31, the Sisters recorded in their daily chronicle that the Convent Hospital was almost deserted:

> Major Hall received an order to send all of our sick who were off the list of combatants because of their illness, and also those whose sickness calls for long treatment. A large number embarked on the ship *Solace* which will leave our port this evening or tomorrow for New York; there they will be transferred to the Brooklyn Hospital. Some others who have been ill but are cured will return to their respective ships. Of the sixty patients we had yesterday only about 15 remain.

The Convent of Mary Immaculate was converted into an army hospital during the Spanish-American War. Built on Division Street (today's Truman Avenue) in 1878, the Convent with its outlying buildings and tents could take care of as many as 500 men. The graceful structure was torn down in 1968.

During June, only a few patients were admitted to the Convent Hospital. Most were not suffering from combat wounds, but from a variety of ailments—including alcoholism, falls, measles, hernias, heat stroke, and malaria.

On June 2, 1898, Commander Forsyth, as Commandant of the Naval Station, Key West, petitioned the Mayor and Board of Aldermen on behalf of the government for permission "to enclose a certain piece of ground in the City Cemetery, on the plot where the men of the *U.S. Ship Maine* are buried, and also to take in the graves, in the back, of the men of the Army and Navy of that late Civil War. The piece of ground is 58 ft. x 90 ft. and the enclosure will be an iron fence from three to four feet high." The mayor appointed a committee composed of Aldermen Allen. E. Curry, Charles R. Pierce, and Lawrence Higgs to confer with Commander Forsyth.

Although Tampa was the port of departure for most U.S. troops going to Cuba, Key West served as a "jumping-off spot" for many. The water shortage due to the drought kept more troops from being sent here. To accomodate those that did come, tents were set up all over government property and the South Beach area. Physicians proclaimed that "considering the season and the fact that the island is crowded with strangers, Key West is remarkably healthy!"

Extra mail carriers were brought in from Jacksonville, Florida to handle the heavy flow of mail and they even delivered on Sunday mornings to cover the city. The out-of-town carriers said it would take them a while to find all the places and alleys in Key West.

Despite the war-time boom, the Key West economy remained dependent on the sea. Although fishermen could no longer sell their catch in Havana, demand by the military and others helped fill the void. Figures for the 1898 catch are not available, but they are believed to have been comparable to that of 1895 when a survey noted that "92 smackees caught 2.4 million pounds, including almost 605,000 pounds of grunts, 420,000 pounds of king mackerel, 190,000 pounds of mutton snapper and 157,000 pounds of spiny lobster." Big as it was, however, fishing came in second to sponging. The *Florida Times-Union* noted "the sponge industry still forms the chief source of revenue, but at such times as these everyone is doing business."

Even the cigar-makers were "doing business." Although shipments of tobacco from Cuba had stopped with the hostilities, the production of cigars in Key West did not decrease noticeably. This was due to most of the manufacturers having sizeable reserves of tobacco stored in their warehouses when the war began.

Jack's Saloon at Simonton and Front Streets was one of the many bars which offered off-duty sailors and soldiers the "Finest Brands—Wines, Liquors & Cigars." One reporter described the Key West saloons as "places which keep open house night and day. Old, seasoned seamen and young, beardless boys crowd around the bars, saloons and dives, and reel away from them bereft of sense and manhood." Jack's Saloon later became the Coca-Cola Bottling Co.

During the second week of June, the drought finally ended with a heavy shower. "Pure drinking water is no longer 'doled out' by the thimbleful," the *Times-Union* noted.

Clara Barton and her party finally left Key West on June 20. The *State of Texas*, stocked with food and medicines, sailed under the protection of the navy for Santiago on the southern coast of Cuba. Here the largest battle of the war was shaping up.

By the end of June navy ships had bottled up Admiral Cervera's fleet in the harbor and U.S. troops had surrounded the city on land. In battles over several days beginning in late June and early July many were wounded and killed. Hundreds of soldiers wounded at the battles of El Caney and San Juan Hill were brought to Key West for treatment at the Convent Hospital.

Starting July 4, a steady flow of over 300 enlisted men and 20 officers streamed into the Convent Hospital following the battle of Santiago. Tents were set up around the Convent to handle the surge of sick and wounded. Prior to the battles, the army had also constructed two frame buildings behind the Convent for the wounded These structures would later be used as the music room and for kindergarten. St. Francis Xavier School and St. Joseph School buildings were also converted into convalescent wards and used for storage of supplies.

The number of wounded was so great that men were transported from ships to the Convent Hospital by mule-powered street cars. The wounded were carried on stretchers from ships moored at the government wharf to the front of the Custom House. Here they were loaded onto the street cars which took them to the Convent.

Stereographs, photographs taken with a twin-lens camera, were popular during the Spanish-American War, and many were taken in Key West. When viewed with a stereoscope, the double photograph gave the viewer the impression of a 3-D image. The photographer snapped this view of the wounded from the battle of Santiago on the steps of the Convent.

VIII

End of the War

Three months and 22 days after it had been declared, the Spanish-American War was over. A peace protocol ending the fighting was signed in Washington on August 12, 1898.

In Key West, the news of that particular day was the weather—not the ending of the war. The *Florida Times-Union* reported that the heaviest rain and thunderstorms to hit Key West in years caused disasters on land and sea. Several sailing vessels were reported lost at sea and lightning severely damaged the Cuban Methodist Church, the Good Templars' Hall and Pat McKuen's saloon. Another strike hit a small house, temporarily paralyzing a woman.

The big celebration took place a few days later when the navy blew up the mines in the harbor. Crowds gathered on the docks and "the whole island shook as large jets of water were thrown far above the masts of vessels in the harbor."

Ships that had blockaded Cuba began returning to Key West. "Naval officers are unanimous in their expressions of gratification that the war is over and are anxiously looking for orders which will take them North," a newspaper noted. Unfortunately for Key West, those orders were issued more quickly than they should have been. This was due to a young medical officer's faulty diagnosis of three cases of fever in a Marine unit.

The inexperienced doctor called it yellow fever, and notified the Secretary of the Navy. On August 16 the order came down to evacuate Key West. Dr. Porter protested, and Dr. William Murray of the Marine Hospital and Dr. A. H. Glennan of the Public Health Service joined him in stating that the fever was dengue, a non-fatal, ten-day fever—not the dreaded, often-fatal yellow fever. It was to no avail. Evacuation started immediately. According to author William J. Schellings:

> The ships in the harbor began taking aboard all shore personnel of the Navy, together with many of the civilian

workers and left port, headed toward Hampton Roads. One company of Marines was left behind as a guard, and even that was removed shortly after. Six days later the Army followed suit, and by August 22 the only uniforms to be seen in Key West were those of the Marines and of a small guard detachment of the soldiers.

Heading north also were the wounded. The Sisters poignantly recorded the closing of the Convent Hospital:

> Last Wednesday [August 17], all the sick sailors bade us a last good-by. The *Lancaster* took them on board to bring them to New York. This morning it is the turn of the soldiers and the hospital personnel. Nurses, doctors, as well as the sick, all seemed loathe to leave our hospital, of which, they say, they will always have the fondest memories. The sailors, in good sea language, said it was the best ship they ever were on. The soldiers claimed that no camp compared to it. These testimonies of gratitude chosen out of thousands prove to us once again that the flower of gratitude grows in all climates and in all locations when hearts are generous and noble.
>
> At about nine o'clock the wards of the sick were deserted, the last ambulance left our door; and from the hall where we had so often welcomed the sick, we now bade good-by to our dear patients.
>
> Since the twenty-second of April when Major R. W. Hall took possession of our Convent in the name of the government to transform it into a hospital, until today, we can but felicitate ourselves on our relations with the thirteen physicians who made up the medical corps; they always treated us with the greatest politeness, and sincerely appreciated our least

W. Dalton O'Neil, a sailor aboard the monitor Puritan *gave this photograph to Sister Thomas at the Convent. After his discharge from the Navy, O'Neil wrote a letter dated February 21, 1899, to the sister expressing "my gratitude for the nursing and exceptionally fine treatment received at the convent hospital."*

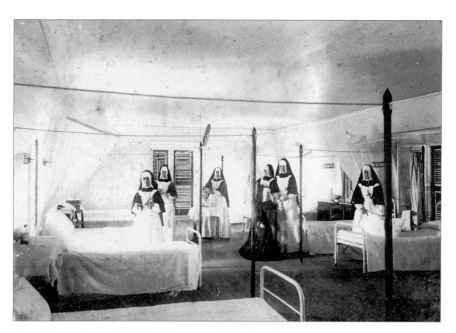

The Convent Hospital had to be dismantled when the war was over, and the school prepared for students. Classes resumed December 1, 1898, but enrollment dropped drastically because many of the Cuban students returned home after the war.

services. A most cordial understanding existed between us and the the fifty-eight secular nurses of both sexes who shared with us the work of caring for the sick. It would take volumes to record all the spontaneous tributes of gratitude received from the five hundred fifty-one soldiers and sailors who came under our care either at the Convent or in the schools. Let it suffice to quote one poor sailor who returned to the practice of religion after many years of negligence: "My stay at the Convent has been my salvation." Several of his companions could have said the same. "How many mothers will bless you for all the good you have done for us!"

What had been a bustling economy came to a halt overnight. Following the lead of the military, states and ports as far away as Louisiana quarantined Key West. When the three sailors fully recovered from the fever in the ten-day period, the navy began to reconsider the diagnosis and finally admitted they might have been wrong. On September 12, navy ships began returning to the city. The army soon followed, and life began to assume a sense of normalcy although it would be some time before all the quarantines were lifted.

Work gradually resumed on unfinished government projects. With funding that had been approved during the war, the navy completed warehouses and repair facilities along the waterfront. and planned new ones. When completed later in 1898, Building 7 would be the "largest, finest, best-equipped, up-to-date machine shop in the South." Two hundred feet long by 60 feet wide, the iron and brick building cost $40,000. Today Building 7 has been rehabilitated and converted into housing units. Building 21, a similar brick structure was planned as a sail and rigging loft, electrical workshop, and equipment storehouse. It was completed in October 1902 at a cost of $50,000; today it is the corporate headquarters of Historic Tours of America.

It has been estimated that the army and navy spent over $2,244,850 on construction in Key West between March 1898 and July 1899. Much of the construction such as the warehouses, docks, and dredging of the channel behind the Naval Depot improved the port facilities. Those improvements would prove of lasting value to the military and the community.

In September the first shipment of tobacco since the beginning of the war was received from Cuba, and the cigar industry began getting back to normal. Cuban refugees who had fled to Key West began returning to their homeland. Ships that had formerly hauled men and weapons as filibusters, were now busy hauling passengers and freight.

The public schools reopened in early October—Sears School (white) had 536 students; Russell Hall (white), 243; Douglass School (colored), 234; and Monroe School (colored), 214.

The Catholic schools at the Convent could not open until December 1 because the hospital had to be disassembled, and repairs and painting were necessary before classrooms could be set up again. In December the nuns noted that "the Cubans, ordinarily so numerous, are hardly represented this year. The freedom of their nation, won by the Americans, has inspired the majority to return to their native land, and this has greatly decreased our classes." Only 120 of 600 students returned.

On December 11, the *Maine* plot in the cemetery was dedicated. A procession from the city hall on Greene Street marched to the cemetery and lined up around the new wrought-iron fence. After the speeches, the flag-raising took place. The *Florida Times-Union* reported:

> The flag raised was the one which went down with the *Maine* in the harbor of Havana while the flag staff upon which it was raised was the mast of the torpedo boat *Winslow*. It was raised by an old sailor from the *Maine*.
>
> The decoration of the graves by the children followed. Fully

eight hundred children were there and each carried a wreath or bouquet or flowers which they placed upon the graves.

For the people of Key West the memorable dedication of the Maine plot came as the year 1898 ended in peace. The day before, the official peace treaty was signed in Paris. Under its terms, Puerto Rico, Guam, and the Philippines were ceded to the United States and Spain relinquished control over Cuba.

The "Splendid Little War" was over.

Looking westerly down Whitehead Street from the lighthouse, the tops of Bethel A. M. E. Church and the Monroe County Courthouse can be seen in the distance in this view of Key West taken at the time of the Spanish-American War.

Oar in hand, a sailor stares out to sea atop the Maine monument. The statue, whose sculptor was Alphons Pelzer, was a "standard sailor figure" made of sheet bronze by the W. H. Mullins Company of Salem, Ohio. In addition to making such things as statues and metal store fronts, the Mullins Company made decorations for the Congressional Library in Washington, D.C. and some of the Naval Academy buildings at Annapolis.

A tremendous crowd attended the dedication of the Maine monument at the city cemetery March 15, 1900. Inscribed at the base of the monument is the following: IN MEMORY OF THE VICTIMS OF THE DISASTER OF U.S. BATTLESHIP 'MAINE' IN HAVANA HARBOR FEB. 15, 1898. ERECTED BY CITIZENS OF KEY WEST, FLA. Townspeople collected funds for two years to pay for the monument.

IX

Monuments & Memories

Following the war, life resumed at a calmer pace but the war was not forgotten. Citizens continued their fund-raising efforts in hopes of purchasing a permanent memorial to be placed in the *Maine* plot in the middle of Key West City Cemetery. When enough was collected, the monument was ordered and a celebration planned. Finally, the great day of dedication came on March 15, 1900. The *Florida Times-Union* reported:

> The unveiling of the monument dedicated by the citizens of Key West to the heroes of the battleship *Maine*, who died in Havana, February 15, 1898, and were buried here, took place this afternoon. Over ten thousand persons were present and viewed the procession, which assembled at the naval station and proceeded to the cemetery. It was headed by the Key West Cornet Band, which was followed by a detachment from the gunboat *Machias*, ordered here by the Navy Department, two companies, B and N, of the first artillery regulars, representatives of the army and navy and city officials in carriages; Key West Guards, Knights of Pythias, Knights of the Golden Eagle, Red Men, and hundreds of school children. The procession was under the command of Col. F. C. Brossier and Grand Marshal B. P. Baker. At the cemetery Mayor Bartlum presided , and introduced the senior chaplain of the navy, Alfred LeRoyce, who offered a fervent prayer.
>
> Col. George Patterson, in behalf of the monument committee, presented the monument to Commander Impey, for the Navy Department, when the band played the Star Spangled Banner, and the flag was unfurled from the monument. Loud cheers greeted the unveiling.

Rev. Charles W. Frazer, orator of the day, made an eloquent address, followed by a benediction by Chaplain LeRoyce. After the unveiling ceremonies, hundreds of school children covered the graves with wreaths and flowers.

Today 24 victims of the *Maine's* explosion lie buried in the plot; seven are identified and 17 are marked "unknown.' Those identified are ordinary seaman Frank Andrews, first class apprentice Benjamin H. Herriman, mess attendant James Pinkney, chief machinist William Rushworth, mess attendant Kashitaro Suzuki, coal passer John H. Ziegler, and U.S. Marine Corps private Edward B. Suman.

Remains of other dead from the *Maine* may also be buried in the plot. Captain Sigsbee's records indicate that Marine First Sergeant Henry Wagner and Boatswain Mate 2nd Class John Anderson are buried in the plot, but their graves cannot be found. Not all of the Spanish-American war veterans buried in the *Maine* plot are from the *Maine*, however. Ernest Sulzesich, a sailor aboard the cruiser *Marblehead*, is buried there. He was wounded while cutting underwater telegraph cables at Cienfuegos and hospitalized in the Army Hospital, but died May 14, 1898.

Joseph A. Acosta, Key West's last veteran of the Spanish-American War, was honored at services held at the Maine plot February 1976 by Southernmost Post 3911 Veterans of Foreign War. Acosta died at the age of 102 and was buried in the Maine plot.

On November 5, 1931, Captain Charles Silva died in the Marine Hospital in Key West and was buried in the *Maine* plot. The 68-year-old captain had help run guns to Cuba prior to the war, and had been a shipmate of Napoleon Bonaparte Broward and "Dynamite" Johnny O'Brien on the filibustering vessel, *Three Friends.* When war came, Silva became a harbor pilot for the navy and was aboard the flagship *New York* at the battle of Santiago.

Joseph A. Acosta, Monroe County's oldest Spanish-American War veteran, is also buried in the *Maine* plot. He died

November 29, 1976 at the age of 102. Acosta joined the U.S. Army in Tampa when he was only 14 and served as an interpreter for Cuban General Máximo Gómez. According his obituary in the *Key West Citizen*, he was among the men who charged up San Juan Hill with Col. Theore Roosevelt.

Over the years the *Maine* plot has been maintained by the U.S. Navy as a military cemetery. In preparation for the centennial anniversary of the sinking of the *Maine*, the navy had the fence, gate, and monument from the plot removed in September 1997 for restoration. Prior to this, the last significant work on the plot was in 1938, with some minor work performed in 1961.

In 1908, on the tenth anniversary of the sinking of the *Maine*, a gun-sighting hood from the battleship was placed on a concrete base at Margaret and Southard Streets on the grounds of Harris School.

The local chapter of the Patriotic Order Sons of America, put a marble marker beneath the hood which read: "This Relic Is Preserved by/Washington Camp/No. 12 P. O. S. of A./In Remembrance of the Battleship *Maine*/Blowing Up in Havana Harbor/February 15, 1898."

Frederick W. Alexander of Oakgrove, Virginia was the speaker at the dedication of the marker. Alexander was voted national President of the P. O. S. of A. in 1909, and campaigned successfully for Congressional funds to raise the *Maine*.

Over seventy years later, in order to preserve the hood which was tilting from tree roots lifting up the concrete base, the Historic Key West Preservation Board received permission from the District School Board of Monroe County to move the hood to the new Post Office at 400 Whitehead Street. A ceremony commemorating the relocation of the gun sighting hood was held February 15, 1985.

In 1910, Congress appropriated $300,000 (a sum more than to triple later) to salvage the *Maine* and recover the remains of

A gun-sighting hood from the battleship **Maine** *stood in the school yard of Harris School from February 1908 until it was moved in 1985. Sailors looked out from slits in the hood to line up the guns on the battleship with their targets.*

A cofferdam was built around the Maine *and the water was pumped out so the battleship could be refloated. In this 1911 photograph, the* Maine *emerges from the bottom of Havana Harbor after 14 years. Investigation of the wreckage confirmed the conclusion of the Court of Inquiry that an external explosion caused the sinking. The* Maine *was towed to sea and sunk again March 16, 1912.*

the crew. With increasing traffic in Havana harbor, the ship had also become a hazard to navigation. A cofferdam was built around the sunken ship, the water pumped out and the ship patched so she could be refloated.

In March 1912, the 66 bodies recovered from the *Maine* were returned to the United States. None, however, were buried in Key West. Sixty-five were interred at Arlington National Cemetery and the only body identified, that of assistant engineer Darwin M. Merritt, was buried in his hometown of Red Oak, Iowa.

Before the patched-up hull of the battleship *Maine* was towed out to sea on the afternoon of March 16, 1912, "Dynamite" Johnny O' Brien who was chief of the Havana harbor pilots and former captain of the filibusters *Dauntless* and *Three Friends*, was put aboard the barnacle-encrusted battleship to guide the procession out to sea. O'Brien later recalled:

> From the masthead floated the Stars and Stripes, the

biggest and handsomest Navy ensign I think I ever saw . . . As I stood alone under the colors there came to me a sudden realization of the wonder of this ceremony in which I was taking part, the like of which the world had never seen nor was likely to see again. I looked across the desolate deck, and there rose in my mind a picture of it bristling with cannon and crowded with strong sailormen and I never felt so much like crying in my life.

The Convent Museum was started soon after the Spanish-American War ended by Sister Mary Egidius who had been in charge of a ward during the war. Various articles from the *Maine*, together with letters and gifts from former patients at the Convent Hospital formed the nucleus of the museum's collection.

When the old Convent was demolished in 1968, many artifacts from the Convent Museum, including those from the Spanish-

The Convent Museum contained a treasure-trove of artifacts from the Spanish-American War. Most of the war-related items were given to the Sisters by grateful soldiers and sailors who had been patients at the Convent Hospital. The museum also housed a large collection of rocks, minerals, and sea shells.

Joe Pais, vice chairman of the U.S.S. Battleship Maine Centennial Commission, addresses the first meeting of the commission February 15, 1995. Nationwide in scope, the commission coordinated commemorations of the 100th anniversary of the sinking of the Maine. The historic meeting was held in the same room on the second floor of the Custom House where the Court of Inquiry met in 1898.

American War,. were loaned to the Key West Art and Historical Society where the collection is today.

The red brick Custom House and Post Office continued its multi-purpose use as a federal building until the early 1930s when a new facility was built at Simonton and Caroline Streets. The old structure was converted into a naval administration building in 1932 and continued throughout World War II to handle civilian personnel affairs. The stately building was boarded-up in 1974 when the U.S. Naval Station was decommissioned.

Eventually the State of Florida acquired it and in 1992 awarded the Key West Art and Historical Society a 99-year lease on the vacant building. A multi-million-dollar restoration of the building was started shortly thereafter, and today a state-of-the-art museum and archive are being created in the 1891 Romanesque Revival brick structure. The Society plans to move most of its operation from East Martello to the Custom House in the spring of 1999. A permanent exhibit on the war and the battleship *Maine* is planned.

A very important chapter in Key West history, the Spanish-American War will not be forgotten.

This commemorative scroll was published in 1898, one of many items manufactured in the rush of patriotism following the sinking of the Maine.

BIBLIOGRAPHY

BOOKS

Blow, Michael. *A Ship To Remember–The Maine and the Spanish-American War*. New York: William Morrow and Co., Inc., 1992.

Browne, Jefferson B. *Key West–The Old and The New*. Gainesville: University of Press, 1973. Facsimile reproduction of the 1912 edition.

Davis, Richard Harding. *The Cuban and Porto Rican Campaigns*. New York. Charles Scribners's Sons. 1898.

Hawk, Robert. *Florida's Army–Militia/State Troops/National Guard 1565-1985*. Englewood, Florida. Pineapple Press, Inc. 1986.

Liebman, Malvina W. and Seymour B. Liebman. *Jewish Frontiersmen—Historical Highlights of Early South Florida Jewish Communities*. Miami: Jewish Historical Society of South Florida, Inc.

Musser, Charles. Vol. 1 of *The Emergence of Cinema: The American Screen to 1907*. Berkeley: University of California Press, 1994.

O'Toole, G. J. A. *The Spanish War–An American Epic–1898*. New York: W. W. Norton & Company, 1984.

Pais, Joseph G. *The Battleship Maine–A Key West Legacy*. Key West: U.S. Battleship Maine Centennial Commission, 1997.

Poyo, Gerald E. *"With All, and for the Good of All"–The Emergence of Popular Nationalism in the Cuban Communities of the United States, 1848-1898*. Durham: Duke University Press, 1989.

Proctor, Samuel. *Napoleon Bonaparte Broward–Florida's Fighting Democrat*. Gainesville: University of Florida Press, 1950.

Rickover, H. G. *How the Battleship Maine Was Destroyed*. Annapolis: Naval Institute Press, 1995.

Ronning, C. Neale. *José Martí and the Émigré Colony in Key West.: Leadership and State Formation*. New York: Praeger Publishers, 1990.

Rubens, Horatio S. *Liberty–The Story of Cuba*. New York: Brewer, Warren and Putnam, 1932.

Samuels, Peggy and Harold. *Remembering the Maine*. Washington, D. C.: Smithsonian Institution Press, 1995.

Sigsbee, Charles D. *The Maine–An Account of Her Destruction in Havana Harbor*. New York: De Vinne Press, 1899.

Tebeau, Charlton W. *A History of Florida*. Coral Gables: University of Miami Press, 1971.

Weems, John Edwards. *The Fate of the Maine*. New York: Henry Holt and Company, 1958.

Westfall, L. Glenn. *Key West: Cigar City U. S. A*. Key West: Historic Key West Preservation Board, 1984.

White, Trumbull. *Pictorial History of Our War with Spain For Cuba's Freedom*. Freedom Publishing Co. 1898.

Wright, Marcus J. *Wright's Official History of the Spanish-American War*. Washington, D. C.: War Records Office, 1900.

Reports, Articles, and Pamphlets.

Message from the President of the United States Transmitting The Report of the Naval Court of Inquiry Upon the Destruction of the United States Battle Ship Maine in Havana Harbor, February 15, 1898, Together with the Testimony Taken Before the Court. Washington, D. C.: Government Printing Office, 1898.

Carney, Philip J. *The Maine Memorial or the Maine-Winslow Plot*. Key West: 1992.

England, Howard S., and Ida Barron. *Fort Zachary Taylor*. Key West: 1977.

Elliott Jr., Robert W. "Clara Barton Comes To Key West." *Florida Keys Sea Heritage Journal* 1, No. 3 (Spring 1991): pp. 4-5.

Hambright, Thomas L. *Battleship Maine Plot–Key West Cemetery*. Key West: SAWVA Publishing, 1993.

Little, Jr., Edward J. "A History of the Fishing Industry in the Florida Keys." *The Monroe County Environmental Story*. Big Pine Key, Florida: 1991.

Mickler, J. R. *Key West in World War II*. Key West: U.S. Navy, 1945.

Schellings, William J. "Key West and the Spanish-American War." *Tequesta* XX, 1960: pp. 19-29.

Newspapers and Periodicals

Florida Times-Union. Jacksonville: 1898.

Harper's Weekly. New York: 1898.

Leslie's Weekly. New York: 1898.

Cost of Living—Key West—1898

Wages: average pay for a cigar maker was $15.00 to $30.00 a week. A skilled laborer could earn $4.00 a day; an unskilled laborer, $2.00.

Food, per can: sardines 6¢, baked beans 5¢; per pound: flour 3¢, coffee 2¢, bacon 12¢.

Clothing: men's shirts 25¢ to $1.50 each, pants 75¢ to $5.50, suits $8.00 to $16.00; ladies hats 95¢.

Transportation: a ride on the mule-powered street car to anywhere in the city (over the six miles of track) cost 5¢. A round-trip steamship ticket from Key West to Havana, $20.00; from Key West to Miami, $15.50.

Hotel room: the cost of a room (such as those typically rented by the journalists) was $1.00.

About the Authors

WRIGHT LANGLEY is a journalist and photographer who moved from his home state of North Carolina to Key West in 1965 to work as a reporter for the *Key West Citizen*.

Three years later he became Keys Bureau Chief for the *Miami Herald*—a position he held for over seven years. After directing the Historic Florida Keys Preservation Board for 15 years, he resumed his writing and photography in 1993.

He has co-authored many books: *Yesterday's Key West* and *Yesterday's Florida Keys* with Stan Windhorn, and *Gator History—A Pictorial History of the University of Florida* with Dr. Samuel Proctor.

JOAN KNOWLES LANGLEY is a Key Wester whose two great-grandfathers came over from the Bahamas in the 1830s. Born and raised in Key West, she returned to the island in 1965.

The managing editor of Langley Press, Inc., she is also a writer. Books to her credit include three co-authored with her husband Wright: *Yesterday's Asheville*, a pictorial history of Asheville, N.C.; *Old Key West in 3-D*, a book of stereo views of Key West; and *Key West—Images of the Past*, a pictorial history of Key West.